7/95

W9-CHX-452

FROGS

FROGS

PETER MURRAY

THE CHILD'S WORLD

If you sit quietly by a pond on a warm evening, you'll probably hear the chirping of birds. You might also hear the chattering of a nearby squirrel, the quacking of a mother duck, or the splash of a fish jumping. If it's breezy, you'll hear the wind rustling through the leaves and grass. But mostly, you'll hear the peeping, croaking, and bellowing of frogs. The frogs are calling to each other. They are saying, "Here I am. Look at me! Aren't I a fine frog?"

Spring is the best time to listen for frogs, but you can hear them all summer long. Frogs call by filling their vocal sacs with air, then forcing the air across their vocal cords. Each type of frog has its own call. Tree frogs make a loud trilling, whistling, or peeping sound. Leopard frogs have a snorting, croaking call. Bullfrogs have a deep, booming call that sounds like they are saying, "Jug-o-rum! Jug-o-rum!"

There are hundreds of different types of frogs. The Goliath frog from Africa is almost as big as a football and can weigh ten pounds! Some tree frogs, on the other hand, are less than an inch long. Tree frogs have tiny, sticky pads on their toes that let them cling to smooth leaves or bark. They can even walk on slippery windowpanes!

Like toads and salamanders, frogs are members of an animal group called *amphibians*. All amphibians are cold-blooded. Their body temperature rises and falls with the air or water temperature. On a hot day, a frog cools itself by staying in the water. On a cool day, it might bask in the sunshine to warm itself.

In cold climates, when winter is coming, frogs burrow into mud at the bottom of a pond to hibernate. They stay buried all winter, waiting for spring. When spring arrives, the frogs dig their way back to the surface.

Frogs are born in water, and they must return to water to breed. When a female frog is ready to lay her eggs, she answers a male frog's mating call. Then the male climbs onto her back and waits for her to lay her eggs in shallow water. As she lays the eggs, the male frog fertilizes them.

Sometimes you can find clumps of frogs' eggs near the edges of ponds. A single clump contains thousands of eggs, each surrounded by a layer of clear jelly. In just a few days, the eggs hatch.

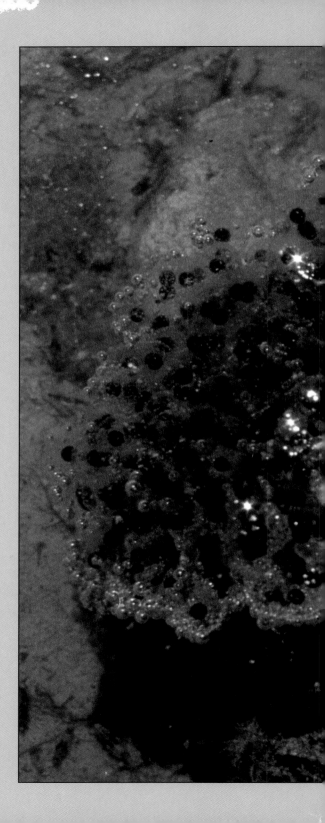

Like most amphibians, frogs live their lives in two stages. The first stage begins when the eggs hatch. The eggs produce tadpoles that look more like little fish than newborn frogs! Tadpoles live underwater, feeding on small water plants. Like fish, they breathe through gills and swim by wiggling their tails back and forth.

Tadpoles have many enemies. Water beetles, fish, birds, and even other frogs like to eat them. Though thousands of tadpoles hatch from one clump of eggs, only a few dozen survive.

Tadpoles grow quickly. When a tadpole is large enough, strange things begin to happen. The tadpole's entire body changes! First, two rear legs begin to grow, one on each side of the tail. Then two front legs pop out through the gill holes. The tadpole's mouth gets wider, its eyes get bigger, and its legs get longer and stronger. The gills that help the tadpole breathe underwater turn into lungs. Now the tadpole must swim to the surface and gulp air to breathe.

The tadpole does not eat while it is changing. Instead, it lives on food stored in its tail. As the tadpole's new legs grow, its tail gets smaller and smaller. Soon, the tadpole is a tadpole no more! It breathes air, not water. It eats insects, not water plants. And it can travel both on land and under-water. Now it is ready to live the second part of its life. The tadpole has changed into a frog.

The young frog faces a whole new world. Now it must hunt for its food! Most frogs feed on insects. They might enjoy a big, juicy June bug for lunch and a bunch of flies for an afternoon snack. To capture its prey, the frog shoots out its long, sticky tongue. Then, when it swallows, the frog blinks its eyes. Its eyeballs help push the food down its throat!

A single frog can eat hundreds of thousands of insects during its lifetime. Imagine how many insects there would be if there were no frogs to eat them!

Not all frogs limit their diet to insects, however. Some eat worms, snails, shrimp, crabs, fish, turtles, and even other frogs! The African bullfrog gobbles mice, rats, birds, and snakes. It sits perfectly still and waits for a small animal to pass by. When one comes close, the frog lunges forward, grabbing the victim in its huge mouth. The frog uses its front feet to push the prey into its mouth. No one can claim that the African bullfrog has good manners!

Frogs are also food for other animals. Turtles, fish, birds, snakes, and raccoons all enjoy a frog for lunch. Even people eat frogs! In France, frogs' legs are considered a delicacy.

Frogs have evolved many ways of defending themselves. They can dive underwater and hide in the mud for hours at a time. Being slippery and hard to hold also comes in handy! And, of course, frogs can jump. A bullfrog can jump twenty times its own length! If it jumps quickly enough to avoid being eaten, a bullfrog can live for twenty years or more.

Besides jumping, one of a frog's best defenses is its coloring. Most frogs have colors and patterns that make them hard to see. If you can't see them, you can't catch them! Tree frogs are often bright green like leaves, or patterned gray and brown like tree bark. Pond frogs are usually green or dull brown, so they blend in with the pond's plants and mud.

Although frogs have many enemies, their greatest threat comes from people. Every year, we drain thousands of ponds, swamps, and marshes and dump millions of gallons of pollutants into rivers and streams. No matter how good their camouflage, how far they jump, and how deep they dive, frogs cannot escape the destruction of their habitat.

We can help frogs survive by preserving our wetlands and keeping the water clean. If we all do our part, our descendants will hear peeping, croaking, and bellowing frogs thousands of years from now.

"Jug-o-rum! Jug-o-rum!"

INDEX

PHOTO RESEARCH

Charles Rotter/Archipelago Productions

PHOTO CREDITS

Leonard Rue III: front cover, 22
Joe McDonald: 2, 28
W. Perry Conway: 4, 24
COMSTOCK/George Porter: 7, 8
Len Rue Jr.: 11
C. Allan Morgan: 12-13
James H. Robinson: 14, 17
Robert & Linda Mitchell: 18, 21, 27
Ralph A. Clevenger: 31

Library of Congress Cataloging-in-Publication Data
Murray, Peter, 1952 Sept. 29-
Frogs / by Peter Murray.
p. cm.
Summary: Describes the physical characteristics, habits,
and life cycle of frogs.
ISBN 1-56766-010-X
1. Frogs--Juvenile literature. [1. Frogs.] I. Title.
QL668.E2M87   1993   92-32499
597.8--dc20   CIP
                                   AC

Distributed to schools and libraries in the United States by
ENCYCLOPAEDIA BRITANNICA EDUCATIONAL CORP.
310 South Michigan Avenue
Chicago, Illinois 60604